FAVORITE BRAND NAME™

Southern
COOKING

Publications International, Ltd.

Favorite Brand Name Recipes at www.fbnr.com

Recipe development on pages 54 and 61 by Marvella Marion-Bowen.

Photography on front cover and pages 25, 55, 57, 59 and 69 by Chris Cassidy Photography, Inc.

Pictured on the front cover *(left to right):* Buttermilk Corn Bread *(page 60)* and Southern Buttermilk Fried Chicken *(page 24).*

Pictured on the back cover *(top to bottom):* Carnation® Key Lime Pie *(page 82),* Ambrosia *(page 58)* and Fried Green Tomatoes *(page 54).*

Microwave Cooking: Microwave ovens vary in wattage. Use the cooking times as guidelines and check for doneness before adding more time.

Preparation/Cooking Times: Preparation times are based on the approximate amount of time required to assemble the recipe before cooking, baking, chilling or serving. These times include preparation steps such as measuring, chopping and mixing. The fact that some preparations and cooking can be done simultaneously is taken into account. Preparation of optional ingredients and serving suggestions is not included.

FAVORITE BRAND NAME™

Southern
COOKING

Southern Cooking

Crispy fried chicken, hush puppies, barbecued ribs and peach pie—they all make your mouth water. And that's just the beginning of what lies in store for you in *Southern Cooking.* This fabulous collection of more than 50 tried-and-true southern recipes is sure to please everyone in your family. Southern cooking will remind you of dinner at Grandma's, a lazy summer afternoon and pitchers of lemonade and sweet tea. It doesn't get much better than that!

Although many people think southern cooking is one cuisine, it is really a collection of many regional cuisines. From Maryland come crab cakes; from Virginia, ham biscuits; from the Carolinas, barbecue and hoppin' John; from Georgia, peach and pecan pies; from Florida, Key lime pie; from the Gulf Coast, shrimp creole and Mississippi mud pie; and from Memphis, barbecued ribs. And all over the South you'll find grits, corn bread, fried chicken, biscuits, fried green tomatoes, collard greens and banana pudding.

Southern cuisine reflects the influence of many groups: Native Americans; early English, Spanish, Irish, Scottish and French settlers; and African and Caribbean natives. Some groups brought foods, such as peaches, red beans, rice, tea, hogs, lemons and turnips; combined with native foods, like corn, sweet potatoes, squash, seafood, pecans and pumpkins, the cuisine of the southern United States was born.

If you've ever lived in or visited the South, you know that southern cooking is more than succulent main dishes and fantastic desserts—it's really all about hospitality. Southerners love to entertain and share a meal; spur-of-the-moment dinner invitations are commonplace in the South but the food is not. Many of a southern cook's recipes have been handed down from generation to generation and shared at church suppers and family reunions; others are more recent additions to her recipe box. However, all of them remind you of a time when the pace was slower, the friendships closer and the food unforgettable.

Start today to share these irresistible southern recipes with your family and friends; soon they will be talking about your wonderful cooking and your warm hospitality.

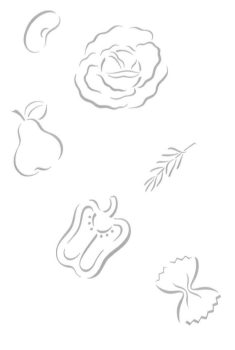

Simple Starters

Baltimore Crab Cakes

Crab is abundant in the waters off Maryland. Crab cakes are a favorite use for crabmeat. In fact, recipes for this appetizer or entrée date back to the eighteenth century.

16 ounces lump crabmeat, picked over and flaked
 1 cup saltine cracker crumbs, divided
 2 eggs, lightly beaten
¼ cup chopped green onions
¼ cup minced fresh parsley
¼ cup mayonnaise
 2 tablespoons fresh lemon juice
 1 teaspoon green pepper sauce
¼ teaspoon salt
   Black pepper
 4 tablespoons vegetable oil
 2 tablespoons butter
   Lemon wedges

1. Combine crabmeat, ¼ cup cracker crumbs, eggs, green onions, parsley, mayonnaise, lemon juice, pepper sauce, salt and pepper to taste in medium bowl; mix well. Shape mixture into 12 cakes, using ¼ cup crab mixture for each.

2. Place remaining ¾ cup cracker crumbs in shallow bowl. Coat crab cakes with cracker crumbs, lightly pressing crumbs into cakes. Place cakes on plate; cover and refrigerate 30 minutes to 1 hour.

3. Heat oil and butter in large skillet over medium heat until butter is melted. Cook crab cakes 3 to 4 minutes or until golden brown on bottoms. Turn and cook 3 minutes or until golden brown and internal temperature reaches 170°F. Serve immediately with lemon wedges. *Makes 12 servings*

Baltimore Crab Cakes

Honey Roasted Ham Biscuits

1 (10-ounce) can refrigerated buttermilk biscuits

2 cups (12 ounces) diced CURE 81® ham

½ cup honey mustard

¼ cup finely chopped honey roasted peanuts, divided

Heat oven to 400°F. Separate biscuits. Place in muffin pan cups, pressing gently into bottoms and up sides of cups. In bowl, combine ham, honey mustard and 2 tablespoons peanuts. Spoon ham mixture evenly into biscuit cups. Sprinkle with remaining 2 tablespoons peanuts. Bake 15 to 17 minutes. *Makes 10 servings*

Peppered Pecans

3 tablespoons butter or margarine

3 cloves garlic, minced

1½ teaspoons TABASCO® brand Pepper Sauce

½ teaspoon salt

3 cups pecan halves

Preheat oven to 250°F. Melt butter in small skillet. Add garlic, TABASCO® Sauce and salt; cook 1 minute. Toss pecans with butter mixture; spread in single layer on baking sheet. Bake 1 hour or until pecans are crisp, stirring occasionally. *Makes 3 cups*

These Peppered Pecans make a temptingly spicy snack. Like most nuts, pecans are high in fat so store leftovers in an airtight container in a cool place for up to 2 weeks.

Honey Roasted Ham Biscuits

Quick Pimiento Cheese Snacks

Pimiento cheese is a favorite among southerners. Here it is served on toasted French bread, but it is also great on crackers and as a stuffing for celery.

  2 ounces reduced-fat cream cheese, softened
  ½ cup (2 ounces) shredded Cheddar cheese
  1 jar (2 ounces) diced pimientos, drained
  2 tablespoons finely chopped pecans
  ½ teaspoon hot pepper sauce
  24 (¼-inch-thick) French bread slices or party bread slices

1. Preheat broiler.

2. Combine cream cheese and Cheddar cheese in small bowl; mix well. Stir in pimientos, pecans and pepper sauce.

3. Place bread slices on broiler pan or nonstick baking sheet. Broil 4 inches from heat 1 to 2 minutes or until lightly toasted on both sides.

4. Spread cheese mixture evenly onto bread slices. Broil 1 to 2 minutes or until cheese mixture is hot and bubbly. Transfer to serving plate; garnish, if desired.

Makes 24 servings

Quick Pimiento Cheese Snacks

Deviled Eggs

12 large eggs, at room temperature
1 tablespoon vinegar
Lettuce leaves

Filling

3 tablespoons *Frank's*® *RedHot*® Original Cayenne Pepper Sauce
2 tablespoons mayonnaise
2 tablespoons sour cream
½ cup minced celery
¼ cup minced red onion
¼ teaspoon garlic powder

1. Place eggs in a single layer in bottom of large saucepan; cover with water. Add vinegar to water. Bring to a full boil. Immediately remove from heat. Cover; let stand 15 minutes. Drain eggs and rinse with cold water. Set eggs in bowl of ice water; cool.

2. To peel eggs, tap against side of counter. Gently remove shells, holding eggs under running water. Slice eggs in half lengthwise; remove yolks to medium bowl. Arrange whites on lettuce-lined platter.

3. To make filling, add *Frank's RedHot* Sauce, mayonnaise and sour cream to egg yolks in bowl. Mix until well blended and creamy. Stir in celery, onion and garlic powder; mix well. Spoon about 1 tablespoon filling into each egg white. Garnish with parsley, capers or caviar, if desired. Cover with plastic wrap; refrigerate 30 minutes before serving.

Makes 12 servings (about 1½ cups filling)

Tip: Filling may be piped into whites through large star-shaped pastry tip inserted into corner of plastic bag.

Prep Time: 40 minutes
Cook Time: 20 minutes
Chill Time: 30 minutes

Praline Pecans & Cranberries

Pecan trees are native to the United States; they are widely grown in Georgia and the Carolinas. Enjoy pecans in snack mixes, desserts and main dishes.

3½ cups pecan halves
¼ cup packed light brown sugar
¼ cup light corn syrup
2 tablespoons butter or margarine
1 teaspoon vanilla
¼ teaspoon baking soda
1½ cups dried cranberries or cherries

1. Preheat oven to 250°F. Grease 13×9-inch baking pan; set aside. Cover large baking sheet with heavy-duty foil; set aside.

2. Spread pecans in single layer in prepared greased baking pan.

3. Combine brown sugar, corn syrup and butter in small microwavable bowl. Microwave at HIGH 1 minute; stir. Microwave 30 seconds to 1 minute or until mixture boils rapidly. Stir in vanilla and baking soda until well blended. Drizzle evenly over pecans; stir until evenly coated.

4. Bake 1 hour, stirring every 20 minutes with spoon. Immediately transfer mixture to prepared foil-covered baking sheet, spreading pecans evenly over foil with lightly greased spatula.

5. Cool completely. Break pecans apart with spoon. Combine pecans and cranberries in large bowl.

6. Store in airtight container at room temperature up to 2 weeks.

Makes about 5 cups

A boiling sugar syrup like the one in step 3 can cause serious burns. Handle it carefully and add the vanilla and baking soda slowly because the syrup may boil up.

Festive Crab Toasts

Crab dishes are popular in the southern states along the Atlantic coast. This sure-to-please appetizer is easy to make.

12 ounces crabmeat, flaked
1 can (10¾ ounces) reduced-fat condensed cream of celery soup, undiluted
¼ cup chopped celery
¼ cup sliced green onions
1 tablespoon lemon juice
⅛ teaspoon grated lemon peel
1 (8-ounce) French bread baguette
⅓ cup grated Parmesan cheese
Paprika

1. Combine crabmeat, soup, celery, green onions, lemon juice and lemon peel in medium bowl; mix well. Cut baguette diagonally into ½-inch slices; arrange slices on 2 ungreased baking sheets. Broil 5 inches from heat 2 minutes or until toasted, turning once.

2. Spread 1 tablespoon crab mixture onto each baguette slice. Top with Parmesan cheese; sprinkle with paprika. Broil 5 inches from heat 2 minutes or until lightly browned.   *Makes about 30 appetizers*

Cheese Straws

These sharp Cheddar "straws" will melt in your mouth.

½ cup (1 stick) butter, softened
⅛ teaspoon salt
Dash ground red pepper
1 pound sharp Cheddar cheese, shredded, at room temperature
2 cups self-rising flour

Heat oven to 350°F. In mixer bowl, beat butter, salt and pepper until creamy. Add cheese; mix well. Gradually add flour, mixing until dough begins to form a ball. Form dough into ball with hands. Fit cookie press with small star plate; fill with dough according to manufacturer's directions. Press dough onto cookie sheets in 3-inch-long strips (or desired shapes). Bake 12 minutes, just until lightly browned. Cool completely on wire rack. Store tightly covered.   *Makes about 10 dozen appetizers*

*Favorite recipe from **Southeast United Dairy Industry Association, Inc.***

Festive Crab Toasts

Main Dish Favorites

Savory Chicken and Biscuits

1 pound boneless, skinless chicken thighs or breasts, cut into 1-inch pieces

1 medium potato, cut into 1-inch pieces

1 medium yellow onion, cut into 1-inch pieces

8 ounces fresh mushrooms, quartered

1 cup fresh baby carrots

1 cup chopped celery

1 (14½-ounce) can chicken broth

3 cloves garlic, minced

1 teaspoon dried rosemary leaves

1 teaspoon salt

1 teaspoon black pepper

3 tablespoons cornstarch blended with ½ cup cold water

1 cup frozen peas, thawed

1 (4-ounce) jar sliced pimientos, drained

1 package BOB EVANS® Frozen Buttermilk Biscuit Dough

Preheat oven to 375°F. Combine chicken, potato, onion, mushrooms, carrots, celery, broth, garlic, rosemary, salt and pepper in large saucepan. Bring to a boil over high heat. Reduce heat to low and simmer, uncovered, 5 minutes. Stir in cornstarch mixture; cook 2 minutes. Stir in peas and pimientos; return to a boil. Transfer chicken mixture to 2-quart casserole dish; arrange frozen biscuits on top. Bake 30 to 35 minutes or until biscuits are golden brown. Refrigerate leftovers.   *Makes 4 to 6 servings*

Savory Chicken and Biscuits

Shrimp Creole

Creole cooking was primarily derived from French and Spanish cuisines, but it was also influenced by native Americans, Africans and immigrants from Italy, Germany and the West Indies. This is a quick and easy version of the best-known creole dish, shrimp creole.

    2 tablespoons olive oil
    1 medium onion, chopped
    1 medium green bell pepper, chopped
    1 jar (1 pound 10 ounces) RAGÚ® Chunky Gardenstyle Pasta Sauce
    ½ cup bottled clam juice
    2 to 3 teaspoons hot pepper sauce
  1½ pounds medium shrimp, peeled and deveined

1. In 12-inch skillet, heat olive oil over medium–high heat and cook onion and green pepper, stirring frequently, 6 minutes or until tender.

2. Stir in Ragú Pasta Sauce, clam juice and hot pepper sauce. Bring to a boil over high heat. Reduce heat to medium and continue cooking, stirring occasionally, 5 minutes. Stir in shrimp and cook, stirring occasionally, 3 minutes or until shrimp turn pink.

3. Serve, if desired, over hot cooked rice.   *Makes 4 servings*

Tip: For a more classic dish, stir in 1 package (9 ounces) chopped frozen okra with Ragú Chunky Gardenstyle Pasta Sauce. Okra is a popular vegetable in the southeastern United States and is used in cooking for thickening and flavor.

Prep Time: 10 minutes
Cook Time: 20 minutes

Shrimp Creole

BBQ Shortribs with Cola Sauce

1 large (17×15 inches) foil bag
    All-purpose flour
1 can (12 ounces) regular cola
1 can (6 ounces) tomato paste
¾ cup honey
½ cup cider vinegar
1 teaspoon salt
2 cloves garlic, minced
    Dash hot pepper sauce (optional)
4 pounds beef shortribs, cut into 2-inch lengths

1. Preheat oven to 450°F. Place foil bag in 1-inch deep jelly-roll pan. Spray inside of bag with nonstick cooking spray. Dust with flour.

2. To prepare sauce, combine cola, tomato paste, honey, vinegar, salt, garlic and pepper sauce, if desired, in 2-quart saucepan. Bring to a boil over medium-high heat. Reduce heat slightly; cook about 15 minutes, stirring occasionally, or until slightly reduced.

3. Dip each shortrib in sauce. Place ribs in single layer in prepared foil bag. Ladle additional 1 cup sauce into bag. Seal bag, leaving headspace for heat circulation, by folding open end twice.

4. Bake 1 hour 15 minutes or until ribs are cooked through. Carefully cut open bag.

Makes 4 to 6 servings

BBQ Shortribs with Cola Sauce

Southern Buttermilk Fried Chicken

3 pounds chicken pieces

2 cups all-purpose flour

1½ teaspoons celery salt

1 teaspoon dried thyme leaves

¾ teaspoon black pepper

½ teaspoon dried marjoram leaves

1¾ cups buttermilk

2 cups vegetable oil

1. Rinse chicken; pat dry with paper towels. Combine flour, celery salt, thyme, pepper and marjoram in shallow bowl. Pour buttermilk into medium bowl.

2. Heat oil in large skillet* over medium heat until oil reaches 340°F on deep-fat thermometer.

3. Dip half the chicken in buttermilk, one piece at a time; shake off excess buttermilk. Coat with flour mixture; shake off excess. Dip again in buttermilk, then coat with flour mixture. Fry chicken, skin side down, 10 to 12 minutes or until brown; turn and fry 12 to 14 minutes or until brown and juices run clear. Drain on paper towels. Repeat with remaining chicken, buttermilk and flour mixture. *Makes 4 servings*

*A cast iron skillet or a heavy deep skillet are good choices for pan-frying.

Tip: Carefully monitor the temperature of the vegetable oil during cooking. It should not drop below 325°F or go higher than 350°F. Chicken may also be cooked in a deep fryer following the manufacturer's directions. Never leave hot oil unattended.

Buttermilk adds a special tang to this fried chicken recipe. Before refrigeration it was common in the warm climate of the South to turn excess milk into butter; buttermilk is a by-product of churning. Southerners often use it in biscuits, corn bread and when making fried foods.

Southern Buttermilk Fried Chicken

Deep South Ham and Redeye Gravy

Country ham and redeye gravy is a traditional southern dish; coffee is the surprise addition to the gravy. Ham steak has been substituted here.

1 tablespoon butter
1 ham steak (about 1⅓ pounds)
1 cup strong coffee
¾ teaspoon sugar
¼ teaspoon hot pepper sauce

1. Heat large skillet over medium-high heat until hot. Add butter; tilt skillet to coat bottom. Add ham steak; cook 3 minutes. Turn; cook 2 minutes longer or until lightly browned. Remove ham to serving platter; keep warm.

2. Add coffee, sugar and pepper sauce to same skillet. Bring to a boil over high heat; boil 2 to 3 minutes or until liquid is reduced to ¼ cup, scraping up any brown bits. Serve gravy over ham.

Makes 4 to 6 servings

Serving Suggestion: Serve ham steak with sautéed greens and poached eggs.

Carolina Baked Beans & Pork Chops

2 cans (16 ounces each) pork and beans
½ cup chopped onion
½ cup chopped green bell pepper
¼ cup *French's® Classic Yellow®* Mustard
¼ cup packed light brown sugar
2 tablespoons *French's®* Worcestershire Sauce
1 tablespoon *Frank's® RedHot®* Original Cayenne Pepper Sauce
6 boneless pork chops (1 inch thick)

1. Preheat oven to 400°F. Combine all ingredients *except pork chops* in 3-quart shallow baking dish; mix well. Arrange chops on top, turning once to coat with sauce.

2. Bake, uncovered, 30 to 35 minutes or until pork is no longer pink in center. Stir beans around chops once during baking. Serve with green beans or mashed potatoes, if desired.

Makes 6 servings

Prep Time: 10 minutes
Cook Time: 30 minutes

Country Captain Chicken

Curry powder in a southern recipe? This dish is believed to have been introduced to Savannah cooks by a sea captain whose travels took him to Asia. Country Captain became popular in the nineteenth century in port cities where there was greater access to imported herbs and spices like Indian curry powder. This version uses a modern slow cooker for ease of preparation.

4 boneless skinless chicken breasts or thighs

2 tablespoons all-purpose flour

2 tablespoons vegetable oil, divided

1 cup chopped green bell pepper

1 large onion, chopped

1 rib celery, chopped

1 clove garlic, minced

¼ cup chicken broth

2 cups canned crushed tomatoes or diced fresh tomatoes

½ cup golden raisins

1½ teaspoons curry powder

1 teaspoon salt

¼ teaspoon paprika

¼ teaspoon black pepper

2 cups hot cooked rice

Slow Cooker Directions

1. Coat chicken with flour; set aside. Heat 1 tablespoon oil in large skillet over medium-high heat until hot. Add bell pepper, onion, celery and garlic. Cook and stir 5 minutes or until vegetables are tender. Place vegetables in slow cooker.

2. Heat remaining 1 tablespoon oil in same skillet over medium-high heat. Add chicken; cook 5 minutes per side or until browned. Place chicken in slow cooker.

3. Pour broth into skillet. Cook and stir over medium-high heat, scraping up any browned bits from bottom of skillet. Pour liquid into slow cooker. Add tomatoes, raisins, curry powder, salt, paprika and black pepper. Cover; cook on LOW 3 hours. Serve chicken with sauce over rice.   *Makes 4 servings*

Chicken Etouffée

Browning flour in a skillet is the secret behind creating a healthy version of this classic Cajun dish. Eliminating the usual roux—a blend of butter and flour—from the recipe removes much of the fat while still allowing the distinctive flavors of the dish to come through.

   Dry Roux (recipe follows)
  4 chicken breasts
 ¾ teaspoon salt
 ½ teaspoon ground red pepper
 ¼ teaspoon black pepper
 1 tablespoon vegetable oil
 3 cups chopped onions
 ½ cup chopped green bell pepper
 1 cup water, divided
 3 large cloves garlic, minced
 3 cups chicken broth
 ¼ cup chopped green onions
  Hot cooked rice

1. Prepare Dry Roux.

2. Remove skin and fat from chicken. Combine salt, red pepper and black pepper in cup; sprinkle 1 teaspoon mixture over chicken. Heat oil in large heavy skillet over medium heat. Add chicken; cover and cook about 20 minutes or until browned on all sides, draining any liquid in pan halfway through cooking time.

3. Remove chicken from skillet. Add onions and bell pepper; cover and cook 5 to 6 minutes or until onions begin to brown, stirring occasionally. Add ⅓ cup water and increase heat to medium-high. Cook about 10 minutes or until mixture begins to stick and brown again, stirring frequently and watching carefully to prevent burning. Add ⅓ cup water; cook and stir until mixture begins to stick and brown again. Add remaining ⅓ cup water and garlic; cook until mixture begins to stick and brown again, stirring frequently.

4. Stir in chicken broth; bring to a boil over medium-high heat. Quickly whisk in Dry Roux until smooth; cook 5 minutes. Add chicken and remaining ½ teaspoon salt mixture to skillet; bring to a boil.

5. Reduce heat to medium-low; simmer about 15 minutes or until mixture is thickened and chicken is no longer pink in center. Sprinkle with green onions. Serve over rice. Garnish with green bell pepper and carrot, if desired. *Makes 4 servings*

Dry Roux: Heat medium skillet over medium heat about 3 minutes. Add ⅓ cup flour to skillet; cook 10 to 15 minutes or until flour turns the color of peanut butter or pale cinnamon, stirring frequently to prevent burning. Sift flour into small bowl; set aside.

Chicken Etouffée

Louisiana Red Beans & Rice

Red beans and rice are a well known New Orleans dish. Stories abound to explain why this favorite dish was traditionally served on Mondays. Two most often repeated stories are these: Monday was typically spent doing laundry and the all-day cooking needed for this dish made it an ideal choice for dinner. Others say it gave cooks the opportunity to use the ham bone left over from Sunday dinner. Here smoked sausage is used to make the dish more filling and canned beans make for quicker preparation.

½ pound smoked sausage (such as kielbasa, chorizo or andouille), cut into thin slices

3 cups cut-up vegetables (onion, bell pepper and celery)

2 cloves garlic, minced *or* ½ teaspoon garlic powder

3 cans (15 to 19 ounces each) red kidney beans, undrained

¼ cup **Frank's® RedHot®** Original Cayenne Pepper Sauce

1 teaspoon dried thyme leaves

2 bay leaves

Hot cooked rice

1. Cook sausage in large nonstick skillet over medium–high heat 5 minutes or until browned. Add onion, bell pepper, celery and garlic. Cook and stir 3 minutes or until vegetables are crisp-tender.

2. Stir in beans, *Frank's RedHot* Sauce and herbs. Heat to boiling. Reduce heat to medium–low. Cook, uncovered, 10 minutes or until flavors are blended, stirring occasionally. Discard bay leaves. Serve over hot cooked rice.   *Makes 6 servings*

Prep Time: 10 minutes
Cook Time: 20 minutes

Louisiana Red Beans & Rice

Southern Fried Catfish with Hush Puppies

Hush puppies didn't appear in southern cookbooks until the twentieth century. Made from corn meal, hush puppy batter is dropped into hot oil and fried.

Hush Puppy Batter (recipe follows)
4 catfish fillets (about 1½ pounds)
½ cup yellow cornmeal
3 tablespoons all-purpose flour
1½ teaspoons salt
¼ teaspoon ground red pepper
Vegetable oil for frying
Fresh parsley sprigs for garnish

1. Prepare Hush Puppy Batter; set aside.

2. Rinse catfish and pat dry with paper towels. Combine cornmeal, flour, salt and red pepper in shallow dish. Dip fish in cornmeal mixture. Heat 1 inch of oil in large, heavy skillet over medium heat until oil registers 375°F on deep-fry thermometer.

3. Fry fish, a few pieces at a time, 4 to 5 minutes or until golden brown and fish flakes easily when tested with fork. Adjust heat to maintain temperature. (Allow temperature of oil to return to 375°F between each batch.) Drain fish on paper towels.

4. To make Hush Puppies, drop batter by tablespoonfuls into hot oil. Fry, a few pieces at a time, 2 minutes or until golden brown. Garnish, if desired.   *Makes 4 servings*

Hush Puppy Batter

1½ cups yellow cornmeal
½ cup all-purpose flour
2 teaspoons baking powder
½ teaspoon salt
1 cup milk
1 small onion, minced
1 egg, lightly beaten

Combine cornmeal, flour, baking powder and salt in medium bowl. Add milk, onion and egg. Stir until well blended. Allow batter to stand 5 to 10 minutes before frying. Makes about 24 hush puppies.

Southern Fried Catfish with Hush Puppies

mp & Ham Jambalaya

...s

...er, chopped

...d pepper

...HMANN'S® Original Margarine

... cleaned and cooked (about 1 pound)

2 cups cubed cooked ham (about 1¼ pounds)

1 (16-ounce) can peeled tomatoes, chopped (undrained)

1 teaspoon natural hickory seasoning

1. Cook and stir onion, bell pepper, garlic and red pepper in margarine in large skillet over medium heat until vegetables are tender.

2. Stir in remaining ingredients. Cook for 10 to 15 minutes or until heated through, stirring occasionally. Serve immediately. *Makes 8 servings*

Prep Time: 30 minutes
Cook Time: 20 minutes
Total Time: 50 minutes

Always devein large and jumbo shrimp because their veins are gritty. To devein, cut a shallow slit along the back of the shrimp with a paring knife; lift out the vein. This is easier to do under cool running water.

Shrimp & Ham Jambalaya

Sausage and Cheese Grits

PAM® No-Stick Cooking Spray
1 pound mild or hot sausage, cooked, crumbled and drained
4½ cups water
¼ teaspoon salt
1½ cups grits
2½ cups shredded Cheddar cheese
3 tablespoons WESSON® Vegetable Oil
1½ cups milk
3 eggs, slightly beaten

1. **Spray** a 13×9×2-inch baking dish with cooking spray. Spread cooked sausage in dish; set aside.

2. **Bring** water and salt to a boil in a large saucepan. Stir in grits; reduce heat. Cook 5 minutes or until thickened, stirring occasionally. Add cheese and oil; stir until cheese has melted. Stir in milk and eggs; blend well. **Spoon grits over sausage.**

3. **Bake**, uncovered, in a preheated 350°F oven 1 hour or until grits have set.

Makes 10 servings

Prep Time: 15 minutes
Cook Time: 1 hour

Sausage Gravy

¼ pound spicy bulk sausage
¼ cup all-purpose flour
2 cups milk
½ teaspoon salt
¼ teaspoon black pepper

1. Cook sausage in medium saucepan over medium heat until browned, stirring to crumble.

2. Drain off all fat except about 2 tablespoons. Stir in flour. Cook, stirring constantly, until thickened and bubbly.

3. Gradually whisk in milk, salt and pepper. Cook, stirring constantly, until thickened and bubbly, about 5 minutes. Serve over biscuits. *Makes about 4 servings*

Newman's Own® Pecan Chicken with Brandied Peach Salsa

⅓ cup gingersnap crumbs (about 6 cookies)
⅓ cup pecans, ground
4 boneless skinless, chicken breast halves
1 tablespoon Dijon mustard
1 (16-ounce) jar NEWMAN'S OWN® Peach Salsa
2 tablespoons peach brandy
¼ cup toasted pecan halves for garnish*

*To toast pecan halves, place in shallow pan in oven for the last 5 minutes that the chicken is baking.

Preheat oven to 425°F. Spray rack in broiling pan with nonstick cooking spray.

Combine gingersnap crumbs and ground pecans in shallow dish. Brush chicken with mustard, then dredge with crumb-nut mixture, coating all sides. Place chicken on rack in broiling pan. Bake chicken 20 minutes.

Meanwhile, in small saucepan heat salsa and peach brandy over medium heat 5 minutes or until heated through.

To serve, place chicken on platter. Spoon hot peach salsa over and around chicken. Garnish with pecan halves.

Makes 4 servings

Hidden Valley® Fried Chicken

This nontraditional buttermilk fried chicken is a tasty version worth trying.

1 broiler-fryer chicken, cut up (2 to 2½ pounds)
1 cup prepared HIDDEN VALLEY® The Original Ranch® Dressing
¾ cup all-purpose flour
1 teaspoon salt
½ teaspoon freshly ground black pepper
   Vegetable oil

Place chicken pieces in shallow baking dish; pour salad dressing over chicken. Cover; refrigerate at least 8 hours. Remove chicken. Shake off excess marinade; discard marinade. Preheat oven to 350°F. On plate, mix flour, salt and pepper; roll chicken in seasoned flour. Heat ½ inch oil in large skillet until small cube of bread dropped into oil browns in 60 seconds or until oil is 375°F. Fry chicken until golden, 5 to 7 minutes on each side; transfer to baking pan. Bake until chicken is tender and juices run clear, about 30 minutes. Serve with corn muffins, if desired. *Makes 4 main-dish servings*

Carolina Barbecue

While there are several styles of barbecue sauce in North Carolina, tomato sauce or ketchup is a common ingredient in the western part of the state.

1 (5-pound) Boston butt roast
2 teaspoons vegetable oil
1½ cups water
1 can (8 ounces) tomato sauce
¼ cup packed brown sugar
¼ cup cider vinegar
¼ cup Worcestershire sauce
1 teaspoon celery seeds
1 teaspoon chili powder
   Salt and black pepper to taste
   Dash hot pepper sauce

Randomly pierce roast with sharp knife. In Dutch oven, brown roast on all sides in hot oil. In mixing bowl, combine remaining ingredients; mix well. Pour sauce over roast and bring to a boil. Reduce heat; cover and simmer 2 hours or until roast is fork-tender. Baste roast with sauce during cooking time. Slice or chop to serve. *Makes 20 servings*

Favorite recipe from **National Pork Board**

Hidden Valley® Fried Chicken

Memphis Pork Ribs

...der

... powder

... dried oregano leaves

...poons paprika

2 teaspoons black pepper

1½ teaspoons salt

4 pounds pork spareribs, cut into 4 racks

Tennessee BBQ Sauce (recipe follows)

1. Combine chili powder, parsley, onion powder, garlic powder, oregano, paprika, pepper and salt in small bowl; mix well. Rub spice mixture onto ribs. Cover; refrigerate at least 2 hours or overnight.

2. Preheat oven to 350°F. Place ribs in foil-lined shallow roasting pan. Bake 30 minutes.

3. Meanwhile, prepare grill for direct cooking. Prepare Tennessee BBQ Sauce. Reserve 1 cup sauce for dipping.

4. Place ribs on grid. Grill, covered, over medium heat 10 minutes. Brush with sauce. Continue grilling 10 minutes or until ribs are tender, brushing with sauce occasionally. Serve reserved sauce on the side for dipping. *Makes 4 servings*

Tennessee BBQ Sauce

3 cups prepared barbecue sauce

¼ cup cider vinegar

¼ cup honey

2 teaspoons onion powder

2 teaspoons garlic powder

Dash hot pepper sauce

Combine all ingredients in medium bowl; mix well. Makes about 3½ cups sauce.

Memphis Pork Ribs

Carolina-Style Barbecue Chicken

This spicy barbecue sauce made with mustard is used to marinate the chicken pieces and to baste with during grilling. The chicken is served with a slightly sweeter version of the barbecue sauce that has been boiled briefly to thicken it.

2 pounds boneless skinless chicken breast halves or thighs

¾ cup packed light brown sugar, divided

¾ cup *French's*® Classic Yellow® Mustard

½ cup cider vinegar

¼ cup *Frank's*® *RedHot*® Original Cayenne Pepper Sauce

2 tablespoons vegetable oil

2 tablespoons *French's*® Worcestershire Sauce

½ teaspoon salt

¼ teaspoon black pepper

1. Place chicken in large resealable plastic food storage bag. Combine ½ cup brown sugar, mustard, vinegar, *Frank's RedHot* Sauce, oil, Worcestershire, salt and pepper in 4-cup measure; mix well. Pour 1 cup mustard mixture over chicken. Seal bag; marinate in refrigerator 1 hour or overnight.

2. Pour remaining mustard mixture into small saucepan. Stir in remaining ¼ cup sugar. Bring to a boil. Reduce heat; simmer 5 minutes or until sugar dissolves and mixture thickens slightly, stirring often. Reserve for serving sauce.

3. Place chicken on well-oiled grid, reserving marinade. Grill over high heat 10 to 15 minutes or until chicken is no longer pink in center, turning and basting once with marinade. *Do not baste during last 5 minutes of cooking.* Discard any remaining marinade. Serve chicken with reserved sauce. *Makes 8 servings*

Prep Time: 15 minutes
Marinate Time: 1 hour
Cook Time: 10 minutes

Carolina-Style Barbecue Chicken

Hearty Soups
& Stews

Hoppin' John Soup

Hoppin' John, made from black-eyed peas and rice, is traditionally served on New Year's Day in South Carolina low country (coastal region) to bring good luck and prosperity. This spicy version is actually a soup that is updated with canned black-eyed peas.

    4 strips uncooked bacon, chopped

    1 large onion, chopped

    2 cloves garlic, minced

    2 cans (15 ounces each) black-eyed peas, undrained

    1 can (14½ ounces) reduced-sodium chicken broth

    3 to 4 tablespoons *Frank's*® *RedHot*® Original Cayenne Pepper Sauce

    1 teaspoon dried thyme leaves

    1 bay leaf

    2 cups cooked long-grain rice (¾ cup uncooked rice)

    2 tablespoons minced fresh parsley

1. Cook bacon, onion and garlic in large saucepan over medium–high heat 5 minutes or until vegetables are tender.

2. Add peas with liquid, broth, *½ cup water*, *Frank's RedHot* Sauce, thyme and bay leaf. Bring to a boil. Reduce heat to low; cook, covered, 15 minutes, stirring occasionally. Remove and discard bay leaf.

3. Combine rice and parsley in medium bowl. Spoon rice evenly into 6 serving bowls. Ladle soup over rice.   *Makes 6 servings*

Note: For an attractive presentation, pack rice mixture into small ramekin dishes. Unmold into soup bowls. Ladle soup around rice.

Prep Time: 15 minutes
Cook Time: 20 minutes

Hoppin' John Soup

Corn and Tomato Chowder

This chowder takes advantage of the flavor of vegetables that are at their best in summer. The tomatoes are salted to intensify their flavor.

1½ cups peeled and diced plum tomatoes

¾ teaspoon salt, divided

2 ears corn, husks removed

1 tablespoon butter

½ cup finely chopped shallots

1 clove garlic, minced

1 can (12 ounces) evaporated skimmed milk

1 cup chicken broth

1 tablespoon finely chopped fresh sage *or* 1 teaspoon rubbed sage

¼ teaspoon black pepper

1 tablespoon cornstarch

2 tablespoons cold water

Fresh sage sprig for garnish

1. Place tomatoes in nonmetal colander over bowl. Sprinkle with ½ teaspoon salt; toss to mix well. Allow tomatoes to drain at least 1 hour.

2. Meanwhile, cut corn kernels off cobs into small bowl. Scrape cobs with dull side of knife to extract liquid from cobs into same bowl; set aside. Discard 1 cob; break remaining cob in half.

3. Heat butter in heavy medium saucepan over medium-high heat until melted and bubbly. Add shallots and garlic; reduce heat to low. Cover and cook about 5 minutes or until shallots are soft and translucent. Add evaporated milk, broth, sage, pepper and reserved corn cob halves. Bring to a boil over high heat. Reduce heat to low; simmer, uncovered, 10 minutes. Remove and discard cob halves.

4. Add corn with liquid; return to a boil over medium-high heat. Reduce heat to low; simmer, uncovered, 15 minutes more. Dissolve cornstarch in water; add to chowder, mixing well. Stir until thickened. Remove from heat; stir in drained tomatoes and remaining ¼ teaspoon salt. Spoon into bowls. Garnish with additional fresh sage, if desired.

Makes 4 servings

Corn and Tomato Chowder

New Orleans Pork Gumbo

Gumbo, a thick, spicy, stewlike dish popular in New Orleans, includes okra, tomatoes and one or more meats or shellfish. This version begins with a traditional dark roux of butter and flour. Okra, a vegetable brought to America from Africa, adds flavor and thickens the gumbo.

1 pound pork loin roast

  Nonstick cooking spray

1 tablespoon butter

2 tablespoons all-purpose flour

1 cup water

1 can (16 ounces) stewed tomatoes, undrained

1 package (10 ounces) frozen cut okra

1 package (10 ounces) frozen succotash

1 beef bouillon cube

1 teaspoon black pepper

1 teaspoon hot pepper sauce

1 bay leaf

1. Cut pork into ½-inch cubes. Spray large Dutch oven with cooking spray. Heat over medium heat until hot. Add pork; cook and stir 4 minutes or until pork is browned. Remove pork from Dutch oven.

2. Melt butter in same Dutch oven. Stir in flour. Cook and stir until mixture is dark brown but not burned. Gradually whisk in water until smooth. Add pork and remaining ingredients. Bring to a boil. Reduce heat to low and simmer 15 minutes. Remove bay leaf before serving. *Makes 4 servings*

Prep and Cook Time: 30 minutes

New Orleans Pork Gumbo

Chicken and Sweet Potato Ragoût

2 tablespoons vegetable oil, divided
1 (3-pound) chicken, cut into 8 pieces
1 large onion, chopped
1 (14½-ounce) can chicken broth
3 small sweet potatoes, peeled and cut into ¼-inch slices
2 cups shredded green cabbage
1 tablespoon TABASCO® brand Pepper Sauce
1 teaspoon salt
¼ cup water
1 tablespoon flour
¼ cup peanut butter

Heat 1 tablespoon oil in 12-inch skillet over medium heat. Add chicken; cook until well browned. Remove to plate. Add remaining 1 tablespoon oil and onion to skillet; cook 5 minutes. Return chicken to skillet; add broth, potatoes, cabbage, TABASCO® Sauce and salt. Heat to boiling over high heat. Reduce heat to low; cover and simmer 30 minutes or until tender, stirring occasionally.

Combine water and flour in small cup. Gradually stir into skillet with peanut butter. Cook over high heat until mixture thickens. *Makes 4 servings*

Charleston Crab Soup

1½ tablespoons butter
½ cup finely chopped onion
1 tablespoon plus 1½ teaspoons all-purpose flour
1 cup bottled clam juice or chicken broth
2½ cups half-and-half
8 ounces lump crabmeat
1½ teaspoons Worcestershire sauce
½ teaspoon salt
Dash ground white pepper
1 to 2 tablespoons dry sherry

1. Melt butter in medium saucepan over medium-low heat. Add onion; cook and stir 4 minutes or until tender. Stir in flour; cook and stir 1 minute.

2. Add clam juice; cook and stir over medium heat until mixture comes to a boil. Reduce heat to low. Add half-and-half, crabmeat, Worcestershire sauce, salt and pepper. Cook and stir 3 to 4 minutes just until mixture begins to simmer. Remove from heat; stir in sherry. *Makes 4 to 5 servings*

Brunswick Stew

Brunswick County, Virginia, is believed to be the birthplace of Brunswick stew. Originally made of squirrel or rabbit meat, it is now often made with chicken.

2 pounds chicken pieces, rinsed

2⅓ cups cold water, divided

1 can (about 14 ounces) tomatoes, cut-up and undrained

2 large ribs celery, sliced

1 medium onion, chopped

2 cloves garlic, minced

1 bay leaf

½ teaspoon salt

⅛ teaspoon ground red pepper (optional)

6 small unpeeled new potatoes (about ¾ pound), cut in half

1 cup frozen succotash (about ½ of 10-ounce package)

1 cup cubed ham

1 tablespoon all-purpose flour

1. Combine chicken, 2 cups cold water, tomatoes with juice, celery, onion, garlic, bay leaf, salt and red pepper, if desired, in 5-quart Dutch oven. Bring to a boil over high heat. Reduce heat to medium-low; simmer, uncovered, 45 minutes or until chicken is tender, skimming foam that rises to top.

2. Remove chicken from broth and let cool slightly. Discard bay leaf. Skim fat from soup.

3. Remove chicken meat from bones; discard skin and bones. Cut chicken into bite-size pieces.

4. Add potatoes, succotash and ham to Dutch oven. Bring to a boil. Reduce heat; simmer, uncovered, 20 minutes or until potatoes are tender. Stir in chicken.

5. Stir flour into remaining ⅓ cup cold water until smooth. Stir into stew. Cook and stir gently over medium heat until bubbly.   *Makes 6 servings*

New potatoes with either red or brown skins are young potatoes that are dug before they are fully grown. Because their skins are very thin, new potatoes don't need to be peeled.

Spicy Shrimp Gumbo

Gumbo is a hearty stew that many believe was adapted from bouillabaisse, a fish soup favored by early French settlers in Louisiana. Local ingredients, such as pork, andouille sausage, chicken and shrimp, made it uniquely American.

½ cup vegetable oil
½ cup all-purpose flour
1 large onion, chopped
½ cup chopped fresh parsley
½ cup chopped celery
½ cup sliced green onions
6 cloves garlic, minced
4 cups chicken broth or water*
1 package (10 ounces) frozen sliced okra, thawed
1 teaspoon salt
½ teaspoon ground red pepper
2 pounds raw medium shrimp, peeled and deveined
3 cups hot cooked rice
Fresh parsley sprigs for garnish

Traditional gumbo's thickness is like stew. If you prefer it thinner, add 1 to 2 cups additional broth.

1. For roux, blend oil and flour in large heavy stockpot. Cook over medium heat 10 to 15 minutes or until roux is dark brown but not burned, stirring often.

2. Add chopped onion, chopped parsley, celery, green onions and garlic to roux. Cook over medium heat 5 to 10 minutes or until vegetables are tender. Add broth, okra, salt and red pepper. Cover; simmer 15 minutes.

3. Add shrimp; simmer 3 to 5 minutes or until shrimp turn pink and opaque.

4. Place about ⅓ cup rice into each wide-rimmed soup bowl; top with gumbo. Garnish, if desired.

Makes 8 servings

Spicy Shrimp Gumbo

Fried Green Tomatoes

This early fall delicacy may have been a frugal cook's way to use every green tomato before the first frost, but it is now a traditional dish loved throughout the South.

- 2 medium green tomatoes
- ¼ cup all-purpose flour
- ¼ cup yellow cornmeal
- ½ teaspoon salt
- ½ teaspoon garlic salt
- ½ teaspoon ground red pepper
- ½ teaspoon cracked black pepper
- 1 cup buttermilk
- 1 cup vegetable oil
- Hot pepper sauce (optional)

1. Cut tomatoes into ¼-inch-thick slices. Combine flour, cornmeal, salt, garlic salt, red pepper and black pepper in pie plate or shallow bowl; mix well. Pour buttermilk into second pie plate or shallow bowl.

2. Heat oil in large skillet over medium heat. Meanwhile, dip tomato slices into buttermilk, coating both sides. Immediately dredge slices in flour mixture; shake off excess flour mixture.

3. Cook tomato slices in hot oil 3 to 5 minutes per side. Transfer to parchment paper or paper towels. Serve immediately with pepper sauce, if desired. *Makes 3 to 4 servings*

Serving Suggestion: Serve fried green tomatoes with shredded lettuce.

Fried Green Tomatoes

Apple Buttered Sweet Potatoes

This recipe combines much-loved apple butter and sweet potatoes.

1 pound sweet potatoes, cooked, peeled and sliced

1 cup (11-ounce jar) SMUCKER'S® Cider Apple Butter

⅓ cup SMUCKER'S® Pineapple Topping

2 tablespoons butter or margarine, melted

½ teaspoon salt

¼ teaspoon ground cinnamon

¼ teaspoon paprika

Arrange sliced sweet potatoes in ungreased shallow baking dish. Combine apple butter and remaining ingredients; mix well. Drizzle mixture over sweet potatoes.

Bake at 350°F for 20 to 30 minutes or until heated through.   *Makes 6 servings*

Note: If you don't have a shallow dish, you can substitute a casserole. Alternate layers of sweet potatoes and apple butter mixture.

Creamy Coleslaw

½ medium head cabbage, outer leaves removed

¼ cup mayonnaise

2 tablespoons cider vinegar

1 tablespoon plus 1½ teaspoon sugar

¼ teaspoon salt

Black pepper

1. Cut cabbage half into quarters. Cut core from quarters; coarsely shred cabbage into medium bowl using box grater.

2. Combine mayonnaise, vinegar, sugar, salt and pepper to taste in small bowl; mix well. Pour over cabbage; stir until well blended. Cover and refrigerate at least 2 hours or overnight.   *Makes 4 to 6 servings*

Apple Buttered Sweet Potatoes

Ambrosia

This chilled combo of cut-up fruit, miniature marshmallows, coconut and nuts is popular in the South. It is served as a side dish or a dessert.

1 can (20 ounces) DOLE® Pineapple Chunks

1 can (11 or 15 ounces) DOLE® Mandarin Oranges

1 firm, large DOLE® Banana, sliced (optional)

1½ cups DOLE® Seedless Grapes

1 cup miniature marshmallows

1 cup flaked coconut

½ cup pecan halves or coarsely chopped nuts

1 cup vanilla yogurt or sour cream

1 tablespoon brown sugar

• Drain pineapple chunks and mandarin oranges. In large bowl, combine pineapple chunks, mandarin oranges, banana, grapes, marshmallows, coconut and pecans. In 1-quart measure, combine yogurt and brown sugar. Stir into fruit mixture. Refrigerate, covered, 1 hour or overnight.   *Makes 4 servings*

Southern-Style Succotash

Succotash was introduced to early settlers by native Americans, who grew corn and beans together. Since early corn varieties needed special processing, the original succotash was actually hominy and lima beans. This version includes hominy along with corn and beans.

2 tablespoons margarine

1 cup chopped onion

1 package (10 ounces) frozen lima beans, thawed

1 cup frozen corn, thawed

½ cup chopped red bell pepper

1 can (15 to 16 ounces) hominy, drained

⅓ cup fat-free reduced-sodium chicken broth

½ teaspoon salt

¼ teaspoon hot pepper sauce

¼ cup chopped green onion tops or chives

1. Melt margarine in large nonstick skillet over medium heat. Add onion; cook and stir 5 minutes. Add lima beans, corn and bell pepper. Cook and stir 5 minutes.

2. Add hominy, chicken broth, salt and pepper sauce; simmer 5 minutes or until most of liquid has evaporated. Remove from heat; stir in green onion tops.   *Makes 6 servings*

Ambrosia

Buttermilk Corn Bread

2 tablespoons butter

1½ cups cornmeal

½ cup all-purpose flour

1 tablespoon sugar

2 teaspoons baking powder

½ teaspoon salt

½ teaspoon baking soda

1½ cups buttermilk

2 eggs

4 tablespoons butter, melted

¼ cup chopped jalapeño peppers,* or to taste

1 tablespoon finely chopped pimiento

*Jalapeño peppers can sting and irritate the skin; wear rubber gloves when handling peppers and do not touch eyes. Wash hands after handling.

1. Preheat oven to 425°F. Place 2 tablespoons butter in 9-inch square baking dish or quiche pan. Place baking dish in preheated oven just before baking corn bread; heat to melt butter and coat pan.

2. Sift cornmeal, flour, sugar, baking powder and salt into large bowl; set aside. Stir baking soda into buttermilk in medium bowl. Add eggs; beat lightly with fork. Stir in 4 tablespoons melted butter.

3. Add buttermilk mixture, jalapeño peppers and pimiento to cornmeal mixture. Mix just until blended; do not overmix. Pour into heated baking dish. Bake 15 to 20 minutes or until bread is just set. Cut into wedges. *Makes 8 servings*

Note: Corn bread should always be served hot. Do not prepare it until you are just about ready to serve dinner.

Southern Collard Greens

Collard greens belong to the cabbage family. They often grew wild and were harvested during scarce times. Collard greens were originally boiled with fat back, bacon or a ham hock to take the edge off their bitter flavor.

2 bunches collard greens

1 small ham hock

¼ cup apple cider vinegar

¼ cup olive oil

1 small onion, quartered

3 cloves garlic, halved

1 can (about 14 ounces) chicken broth

1 cup water

2 tablespoons butter

Pinch of sugar

Pinch of salt

Pinch of black pepper

1. Wash greens well. Remove and discard stems; coarsely chop leaves. Cover and set aside.

2. Rinse ham hock; place in Dutch oven. Cover with water; add vinegar. Bring to a boil; reduce heat and simmer for 20 minutes. Remove ham hock from Dutch oven; discard liquid. Using same pan, heat olive oil over medium heat until hot. Cook and stir onion and garlic until onion is translucent. Add ham hock, greens, broth and water. Cover; cook over medium heat 1 hour 15 minutes or until greens are tender, stirring occasionally, and adding additional broth or water if needed. Add butter, sugar, salt and pepper; stir until butter melts. *Makes 4 to 5 servings*

Collard greens should be chosen for their crisp, bright and even-colored leaves. Avoid greens that are wilted, yellowed, spotted or have thick, fibrous stems. Collard greens, stored in a plastic bag, will keep for up to five days.

Country Buttermilk Biscuits

2 cups all-purpose flour

1 tablespoon baking powder

2 teaspoons sugar

½ teaspoon baking soda

½ teaspoon salt

⅓ cup shortening

⅔ cup buttermilk*

Or, substitute soured fresh milk. To sour milk, combine 2½ teaspoons lemon juice plus enough milk to equal ⅔ cup in a 1-cup measure. Stir; let stand 5 minutes before using.

1. Preheat oven to 450°F.

2. Combine flour, baking powder, sugar, baking soda and salt in medium bowl. Cut in shortening with pastry blender or 2 knives until mixture resembles coarse crumbs. Make well in center of dry ingredients. Add buttermilk; stir until mixture forms soft dough that clings together and forms ball.

3. Turn out dough onto well-floured surface. Knead dough gently 10 to 12 times. Roll or pat dough to ½-inch thickness. Cut out dough with floured 2½-inch biscuit cutter.

4. Place biscuits 2 inches apart onto *ungreased* large baking sheet. Bake 8 to 10 minutes or until tops and bottoms are golden brown. Serve warm. *Makes about 9 biscuits*

Drop Biscuits: Prepare Country Buttermilk Biscuits as directed in steps 1 and 2, except increase buttermilk to 1 cup. After adding buttermilk, stir batter with wooden spoon about 15 strokes. *Do not knead.* Drop dough by heaping tablespoonfuls, 1 inch apart, onto greased baking sheets. Bake as directed in step 4. Makes about 18 biscuits.

Sour Cream Dill Biscuits: Prepare Country Buttermilk Biscuits as directed in steps 1 through 2, except omit buttermilk. Combine ½ cup sour cream, ⅓ cup milk and 1 tablespoon chopped fresh dill *or* 1 teaspoon dried dill weed in small bowl until well blended. Stir into dry ingredients and continue as directed in steps 3 and 4. Makes about 9 biscuits.

Bacon 'n' Onion Biscuits: Prepare Country Buttermilk Biscuits as directed in steps 1 through 2, except add 4 slices crumbled crisply cooked bacon (about ⅓ cup) and ⅓ cup chopped green onions to flour-shortening mixture before adding buttermilk. Continue as directed in steps 3 and 4. Makes about 9 biscuits.

Country Buttermilk Biscuits, Drop Biscuits, Sour Cream Dill Biscuits and Bacon 'n' Onion Biscuits

Squash Casserole

...elicious creamy casserole that is traditionally topped with ...dinner side dish and is often carried to potluck suppers.

...) condensed cream of chicken or mushroom soup, undiluted
...r (8 ounces) sour cream
...cup (4 ounces) shredded Italian cheese blend
1 cup (4 ounces) shredded Cheddar cheese
1 package (6 ounces) stuffing mix

1. Preheat oven to 350°F. Combine squash, carrot, onion, bell pepper, salt and black pepper in medium saucepan; cover with water. Bring to a boil. Cook 5 minutes or until tender; drain.

2. Combine soup and sour cream in 13×9-inch casserole; mix well. Stir in vegetable mixture and spread evenly. Sprinkle cheeses on top. Top with dry stuffing mix.

3. Bake, covered, 30 minutes or until heated through.   *Makes 6 servings*

Choose small to medium-size summer squash. They should be firm with smooth, glossy unblemished skins.

Summer Squash Casserole

Southern Spoon Bread

Spoon bread is another version of the much-loved southern corn bread. A cross between bread and a soufflé, it is a delicious creamy accompaniment to Sunday dinner.

- 4 eggs, separated
- 3 cups milk
- 1 cup yellow cornmeal
- 3 tablespoons butter
- 1 teaspoon salt
- ¼ teaspoon black pepper *or* ⅛ teaspoon ground red pepper
- 1 teaspoon baking powder
- 1 tablespoon grated Parmesan cheese (optional)

1. Preheat oven to 375°F. Spray 2-quart round casserole with nonstick cooking spray; set aside. Beat egg yolks in small bowl; set aside.

2. Heat milk almost to a boil in medium saucepan over medium heat. Gradually beat in cornmeal using wire whisk. Cook 2 minutes, stirring constantly. Whisk in butter, salt and pepper. Beat about ¼ cup cornmeal mixture into egg yolks. Beat egg yolk mixture into remaining cornmeal mixture; set aside.

3. Beat egg whites in large bowl with electric mixer at high speed until stiff peaks form. Stir baking powder into cornmeal mixture. Stir about ¼ cup egg whites into cornmeal mixture. Gradually fold in remaining egg whites. Pour into prepared casserole; sprinkle with cheese, if desired.

4. Bake 30 to 35 minutes or until golden brown and toothpick inserted into center comes out clean. Serve immediately.

Makes 6 servings

To fold beaten egg whites into cornmeal mixture, with a rubber spatula gently but quickly cut through to the bottom of the bowl and turn ingredients over with a rolling motion. Rotate the bowl a quarter turn each time. Take care not to overmix or the baked spoon bread will not be puffy.

Southern Spoon Bread

Sweet Endings

Bananas Foster

Bananas Foster was created in the 1950's by a New Orleans chef. It was prepared in a chafing dish at the table, then flamed for a spectacular ending. It remains a signature dish.

6 tablespoons I CAN'T BELIEVE IT'S NOT BUTTER!® Spread

3 tablespoons firmly packed brown sugar

4 medium ripe bananas, sliced diagonally

2 tablespoons dark rum or brandy (optional)

Vanilla ice cream

In 12-inch skillet, bring I Can't Believe It's Not Butter!® Spread, brown sugar and bananas to a boil. Cook 2 minutes, stirring gently. Carefully add rum to center of pan and cook 15 seconds. Serve hot banana mixture over scoops of ice cream and top, if desired, with sweetened whipped cream. *Makes 4 servings*

Note: Recipe can be halved.

Choose ripe but still firm bananas for this recipe. They will hold their shape better when cooked.

Bananas Foster

...each Pie

...le Crust (page 72)

...heavy syrup

...lespoons butter or margarine, melted
Additional sugar

1. Heat oven to 400°F.

2. For Filling, drain peaches, reserving 3 tablespoons syrup; set aside. Cut peaches into small pieces; place in large bowl. Combine cornstarch and 3 tablespoons sugar in medium bowl. Add 3 tablespoons reserved peach syrup; mix well. Add remaining sugar, eggs and buttermilk; mix well. Stir in ½ cup melted butter and vanilla. Pour over peaches; stir until peaches are coated. Pour filling into unbaked pie crust. Moisten pastry edge with water.

3. Cover pie with top crust. Fold top edge under bottom crust; flute with fingers or fork. Cut slits or designs in top crust to allow steam to escape.

4. For Glaze, brush top crust with 2 tablespoons melted butter. Sprinkle with additional sugar.

5. Bake at 400°F for 45 minutes or until filling in center is bubbly and crust is golden brown. *Do not overbake.* Cool to room temperature before serving.

Makes 1 (10-inch) pie

Georgia Peach Pie

10-inch Classic Crisco® Double Crust

2⅔ cups all-purpose flour

1 teaspoon salt

¾ CRISCO® Stick or ¾ cup CRISCO® all-vegetable shortening

7 to 8 tablespoons cold water (or more as needed)

1. Spoon flour into measuring cup and level. Combine flour and salt in medium bowl.

2. Cut in ¾ cup shortening using pastry blender or 2 knives until all flour is blended to form pea-size chunks.

3. Sprinkle with water, 1 tablespoon at a time. Toss lightly with fork until dough forms a ball. Divide dough in half.

4. Press dough between hands to form two 5- to 6-inch "pancakes." Flour rolling surface and rolling pin lightly. Roll both halves of dough into circle. Trim one circle of dough 1 inch larger than upside-down pie plate. Carefully remove trimmed dough. Set aside to reroll and use for pastry cut-out garnish, if desired.

5. Fold dough into quarters. Unfold and press into pie plate. Trim edge even with plate. Add desired filling to unbaked crust. Moisten pastry edge with water. Lift top crust onto filled pie. Trim ½ inch beyond edge of pie plate. Fold top edge under bottom crust. Flute. Cut slits in top crust to allow steam to escape. Follow baking directions given for that recipe.   *Makes 1 (10-inch) double crust*

Strawberries & Cream Dessert

1 (14-ounce) can EAGLE BRAND® Sweetened Condensed Milk (NOT evaporated milk)

1½ cups cold water

1 (3½-ounce) package instant vanilla pudding and pie filling mix

2 cups (1 pint) whipping cream, whipped

1 (12-ounce) prepared loaf pound cake, cut into cubes (about 6 cups)

4 cups sliced fresh strawberries

½ cup strawberry preserves

Additional fresh strawberries

Toasted slivered almonds

1. In large mixing bowl, combine EAGLE BRAND® and water; mix well. Add pudding mix; beat until well blended. Chill 5 minutes. Fold in whipped cream.

2. Spoon 2 cups pudding mixture into 4-quart round glass serving bowl; top with half the cake cubes, half the strawberries, half the preserves and half the remaining pudding mixture. Repeat layers of cake cubes, strawberries and preserves; top with remaining pudding mixture. Garnish with additional strawberries and almonds. Chill 4 hours or until set. Store covered in refrigerator.   *Makes 10 to 12 servings*

Mississippi Mud Pie

1 *prepared* 9-inch (6 ounces) chocolate crumb crust

1 cup powdered sugar

1 cup (6 ounces) NESTLÉ® TOLL HOUSE® Semi-Sweet Chocolate Morsels

¼ cup (½ stick) butter or margarine, cut up

¼ cup heavy whipping cream

2 tablespoons light corn syrup

1 teaspoon vanilla extract

¾ cup chopped nuts, *divided* (optional)

2 pints coffee ice cream, softened slightly, *divided*

Whipped cream (optional)

HEAT sugar, morsels, butter, cream and corn syrup in small, *heavy-duty* saucepan over low heat, stirring constantly, until butter is melted and mixture is smooth. Remove from heat. Stir in vanilla extract. Cool until slightly warm.

DRIZZLE *⅓ cup* chocolate sauce in bottom of crust; sprinkle with *¼ cup* nuts. Layer *1 pint* ice cream, scooping thin slices with a large spoon; freeze for 1 hour. Repeat with *⅓ cup* sauce, *¼ cup* nuts and *remaining* ice cream. Drizzle with *remaining* sauce; top with *remaining* nuts. Freeze for 2 hours or until firm. Top with whipped cream before serving.

Makes 8 servings

Eclaire Dessert

3 cups cold milk

2 packages (4-serving size each) vanilla instant pudding mix

1 container (8 ounces) frozen whipped topping, thawed

1 box (32 ounces) graham crackers

1 container (16 ounces) chocolate frosting

1. Beat milk and pudding mix 1 minute in large bowl with electric mixer at medium speed. Fold in whipped topping.

2. Place ⅓ of graham crackers on bottom of 13×9-inch baking dish. Top with ½ of pudding mixture. Repeat layers using ⅓ graham crackers and pudding mixture, ending with remaining graham crackers. Spread frosting over graham crackers. Refrigerate 4 hours or overnight.

Makes 12 servings

Reese's® Peanut Butter and Milk Chocolate Chip Tassies

¾ cup (1½ sticks) butter, softened

1 package (3 ounces) cream cheese, softened

1½ cups all-purpose flour

¾ cup sugar, divided

1 egg, slightly beaten

2 tablespoons butter or margarine, melted

¼ teaspoon lemon juice

¼ teaspoon vanilla extract

1¾ cups (11-ounce package) REESE'S® Peanut Butter and Milk Chocolate Chips, divided

2 teaspoons shortening (do not use butter, margarine, spread or oil)

1. Beat ¼ cup butter and cream cheese in medium bowl; add flour and ¼ cup sugar, beating until well blended. Cover; refrigerate about one hour or until dough is firm. Shape dough into 1-inch balls; press each ball onto bottom and up sides of about 36 small muffin cups (1¾ inches in diameter).

2. Heat oven to 350°F. Combine egg, remaining ½ cup sugar, melted butter, lemon juice and vanilla in small bowl; stir until smooth. Set aside ⅓ cup chips; add remainder to egg mixture. Evenly fill muffin cups with chip mixture.

3. Bake 20 to 25 minutes or until filling is set and lightly browned. Cool completely; remove from pan to wire rack.

4. Combine reserved ⅓ cup chips and shortening in small microwave-safe bowl. Microwave at HIGH (100%) 30 seconds; stir. If necessary, microwave additional 15 seconds at a time, stirring after each heating, until chips are melted and mixture is smooth when stirred. Drizzle over tops of tassies.

Makes 3 dozen cookies

Reese's® Peanut Butter and Milk Chocolate Chip Tassies

Peanut Gems

Peanuts are grown throughout the South. Bakers add them to many recipes including these cookie gems.

2½ cups all-purpose flour

1 teaspoon baking powder

⅛ teaspoon salt

1 cup (2 sticks) butter, softened

1 cup packed light brown sugar

2 eggs

2 teaspoons vanilla

1½ cups cocktail peanuts, finely chopped

Powdered sugar (optional)

1. Preheat oven to 350°F. Combine flour, baking powder and salt in small bowl.

2. Beat butter in large bowl with electric mixer at medium speed until smooth. Gradually beat in brown sugar; increase speed to medium-high and beat until light and fluffy. Beat in eggs, one at a time, until fluffy. Beat in vanilla. Gradually stir in flour mixture until blended. Stir in peanuts.

3. Drop heaping tablespoonfuls of dough about 1 inch apart onto *ungreased* cookie sheets; flatten slightly with fingertips.

4. Bake 12 minutes or until set. Let cookies stand on cookie sheets 5 minutes; transfer to wire racks to cool completely. Dust cookies with powdered sugar, if desired. Store in airtight container.

Makes 2½ dozen cookies

Apple Brandy Praline Pie

Made from brown sugar and pecans, Louisiana praline candy is the inspiration for this apple pie.

   Praline Topping (recipe follows)
¼ cup sugar
 3 tablespoons all-purpose flour
¼ teaspoon salt
 3 eggs
½ cup KARO® Light or Dark Corn Syrup
¼ cup (½ stick) margarine or butter, melted
 2 tablespoons apple or plain brandy
 2 medium apples, peeled and thinly sliced
 1 unbaked (9-inch) pie crust

1. Prepare Praline Topping; set aside.

2. In large bowl combine sugar, flour and salt. Beat in eggs, corn syrup, margarine and brandy. Stir in apples. Pour into pie crust.

3. Sprinkle with topping.

4. Bake in 350°F oven 45 to 50 minutes or until puffed and set. Cool on wire rack.

Makes 8 servings

Praline Topping: In small bowl combine 1 cup coarsely chopped pecans, ¼ cup all-purpose flour, ¼ cup brown sugar and 2 tablespoons softened margarine or butter. Mix with fork until crumbly.

Prep Time: 30 minutes
Bake Time: 50 minutes, plus cooling

*Choose Granny Smith apples for this
scrumptious pie.*

Banana Pudding

Banana pudding is a popular twentieth century dessert; it was originally made from ingredients that cooks had on hand—sugar, cornstarch, milk, eggs, bananas and vanilla wafers. This traditional version is topped with whipped topping.

  60 to 70 vanilla wafers*
   1 cup granulated sugar
   3 tablespoons cornstarch
   ¼ teaspoon salt
   2 cans (12 fluid ounces *each*) NESTLÉ® CARNATION® Evaporated Milk
   2 eggs, lightly beaten
   3 tablespoons butter, cut into pieces
  1½ teaspoons vanilla extract
   5 ripe but firm large bananas, cut into ¼-inch slices
   1 container (8 ounces) frozen whipped topping, thawed

*A 12-ounce box of vanilla wafers contains about 88 wafers.

LINE bottom and side of 2½-quart glass bowl with about 40 wafers.

COMBINE sugar, cornstarch and salt in medium saucepan. Gradually stir in evaporated milk to dissolve cornstarch. Whisk in eggs. Add butter. Cook over medium heat, stirring constantly, until the mixture begins to thicken. Reduce heat to low; bring to a simmer and cook for 1 minute, stirring constantly. Remove from heat. Stir in vanilla extract. Let cool slightly.

POUR *half* of pudding over wafers. Top with *half* of bananas. Layer *remaining* vanilla wafers over bananas. Combine *remaining* pudding and bananas; spoon over wafers. Refrigerate for at least 4 hours. Top with whipped topping.   *Makes 8 servings*

Kentucky Oatmeal-Jam Cookies

½ Butter Flavor CRISCO® Stick or ½ cup Butter Flavor CRISCO® all-vegetable
    shortening plus additional for greasing

¾ cup sugar

1 egg

¼ cup buttermilk*

½ cup SMUCKER'S® Strawberry Jam

1 teaspoon vanilla

1 cup all-purpose flour

½ cup unsweetened cocoa powder

1 teaspoon ground cinnamon

½ teaspoon baking soda

¼ teaspoon ground nutmeg

¼ teaspoon ground cloves

1½ cups quick oats (not instant or old-fashioned), uncooked

½ cup raisins

½ cup chopped pecans (optional)

About 24 pecan halves (optional)

*You can substitute ¾ teaspoon lemon juice or vinegar plus enough milk to make ¼ cup for buttermilk.
Stir. Wait 5 minutes before using.

1. Heat oven to 350°F. Grease baking sheet. Place foil on countertop for cooling cookies.

2. Combine ½ cup shortening, sugar, egg, buttermilk, jam and vanilla in large bowl. Beat at medium speed of electric mixer until well blended.

3. Combine flour, cocoa, cinnamon, baking soda, nutmeg and cloves. Mix into creamed mixture at low speed until blended. Stir in oats, raisins and chopped nuts with spoon.

4. Drop 2 tablespoonfuls of dough in a mound on baking sheet. Repeat for each cookie, spacing 3 inches apart. Top each with pecan half.

5. Bake 10 to 12 minutes or until set. *Do not overbake.* Cool 2 minutes on baking sheet. Remove cookies to foil to cool completely. *Makes about 2 dozen cookies*

Kentucky Oatmeal-Jam Cookies

80 ❧ Sweet Endings ❧

Lime Pie

...ker crumb crust
...Sweetened Condensed Milk
...juice

...l)

...ce in small mixer bowl until combined;
...whipped topping. Refrigerate for 2 hours

Makes 8 servings

Peanut Pie

3 eggs
1½ cups dark corn syrup
½ cup granulated sugar
¼ cup butter, melted
½ teaspoon vanilla extract
¼ teaspoon salt
1½ cups chopped roasted peanuts
9-inch unbaked deep-dish pastry shell

Beat eggs until foamy. Add corn syrup, sugar, butter, vanilla and salt; continue to beat until thoroughly blended. Stir in peanuts. Pour into unbaked pastry shell. Bake in preheated 375°F oven 50 to 55 minutes. Serve warm or cold. Garnish with whipped cream or ice cream, if desired.

Makes 6 servings

Favorite recipe from **Texas Peanut Producers Board**

Carnation® Key Lime Pie

Kentucky Bourbon Pecan Drops

Cookies

    1 cup (2 sticks) butter, softened

    ¾ cup granulated sugar

    ¾ cup packed light brown sugar

    2 eggs

    1 tablespoon bourbon

  2¼ cups all-purpose flour

    1 teaspoon baking soda

    ½ teaspoon salt

    1 cup coarsely chopped pecans, toasted

Chocolate-Bourbon Drizzle

    1 cup semisweet chocolate chips

    1 tablespoon butter

    2 tablespoons heavy cream or half-and-half

    ½ cup sifted powdered sugar

    3 tablespoons bourbon

1. Preheat oven to 350°F. For cookies, beat 1 cup butter and sugars in large bowl of electric mixer at medium speed until light and fluffy. Beat in eggs and 1 tablespoon bourbon.

2. Combine flour, baking soda and salt; gradually add to butter mixture, beating at low speed until dough forms. Beat in pecans.

3. Drop heaping tablespoonfuls of dough 2 inches apart on *ungreased* cookie sheets. Bake 12 to 14 minutes or until set and edges are golden brown. Let cookies stand on cookie sheets 1 minute. Remove cookies to wire racks; cool completely.

4. For drizzle, combine chocolate chips and 1 tablespoon butter in medium microwavable bowl. Microwave at HIGH (100%) 50 seconds; stir well. If necessary, microwave at 10 second intervals until chocolate is completely melted when stirred. Stir cream into chocolate, then powdered sugar; mix well. Stir in bourbon until well blended. Let stand at room temperature until completely cooled.

5. Transfer chocolate mixture to small plastic food storage bag. Cut tiny corner off bag; drizzle decoratively over cookies. Let stand, until chocolate is set.

6. Store tightly covered at room temperature or freeze cookies up to 3 months.

Makes about 2½ dozen cookies

Kentucky Bourbon Pecan Drops

Bread Pudding with Southern Whiskey Sauce

Bread pudding topped with a whiskey sauce is a favorite dessert in New Orleans' restaurants.

½ (1-pound) loaf day-old* French or Italian bread

⅔ cup granulated sugar

⅓ cup packed brown sugar

¾ teaspoon ground cinnamon

¼ teaspoon ground nutmeg

6 eggs

3 cups milk

1 tablespoon vanilla

¾ cup raisins

Southern Whiskey Sauce (recipe follows)

For best results, bread should be slightly stale. If you have fresh bread, cut the bread into ½-inch-thick slices and place them on a tray or a baking sheet. Let them stand at room temperature for 30 to 60 minutes or until slightly dry.

1. Preheat oven to 350°F. Butter 12×8-inch baking dish. Cut bread into ½-inch slices; cut slices into ½-inch cubes to measure 8 cups. Place cubes in prepared baking dish.

2. Combine sugars, cinnamon and nutmeg in large bowl. Beat eggs in medium bowl until frothy; stir in milk and vanilla until blended. Add egg mixture to sugar mixture; stir until well blended. Sprinkle raisins over bread cubes. Pour egg mixture over bread cubes. Push bread into liquid to moisten each piece. Let stand 5 minutes.

3. Bake 45 to 50 minutes or until set and knife inserted into center comes out clean.

4. Prepare Southern Whiskey Sauce. Serve warm sauce over warm bread pudding.

Makes 8 servings

Southern Whiskey Sauce: Combine ¾ cup sugar and 2 teaspoons cornstarch in medium saucepan. Stir in ¾ cup half-and-half or whipping cream; cook and stir over medium-low heat until thick and bubbly. Cook 1 minute more; remove from heat. Carefully stir in 2 tablespoons bourbon whiskey, ⅛ teaspoon ground cinnamon and dash of salt. Cool slightly. Store covered in refrigerator up to two days.

Orange Pecan Refrigerator Cookies

2⅓ cups all-purpose flour
½ teaspoon baking soda
¼ teaspoon salt
½ cup butter or margarine, softened
½ cup packed brown sugar
½ cup granulated sugar
1 egg, lightly beaten
Grated peel of 1 SUNKIST® orange
3 tablespoons freshly squeezed SUNKIST® orange juice
¾ cup pecan pieces

In bowl, stir together flour, baking soda and salt. In large bowl, blend together butter, brown sugar and granulated sugar. Add egg, orange peel and juice; beat well. Stir in pecans. Gradually beat in flour mixture. (Dough will be stiff.) Divide mixture in half and shape each half (on long piece of waxed paper) into roll about 1¼ inches in diameter and 12 inches long. Roll up tightly in waxed paper. Chill several hours or overnight.

Cut dough rolls into ¼-inch slices and arrange on lightly greased cookie sheets. Bake at 350°F for 10 to 12 minutes or until lightly browned. Cool on wire racks.

Makes about 6 dozen cookies

Chocolate Filled Sandwich Cookies: Cut each roll into ⅛-inch slices and bake as directed above. When cool, to make each sandwich cookie, spread about 1 teaspoon canned chocolate fudge frosting on bottom side of 1 cookie; cover with second cookie of same shape. Makes about 4 dozen double cookies.

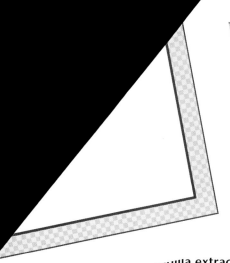

t Potato Pecan Pie

yams, cooked and peeled

rgarine, softened

ND® Sweetened Condensed Milk

...anilla extract

½ teaspoon ground nutmeg

¼ teaspoon salt

1 (6-ounce) graham cracker crumb pie crust

Pecan Topping (recipe follows)

1. Preheat oven to 425°F. In large mixing bowl, beat hot sweet potatoes and butter until smooth. Add EAGLE BRAND® and remaining ingredients except crust and Pecan Topping; mix well. Pour into crust.

2. Bake 20 minutes. Meanwhile, prepare Pecan Topping.

3. Remove pie from oven; reduce oven temperature to 350°F. Spoon Pecan Topping over pie.

4. Bake 25 minutes longer or until set. Cool. Serve warm or at room temperature. Garnish with orange zest twist, if desired. Refrigerate leftovers.   *Makes 1 pie*

Pecan Topping: In small mixing bowl, beat 1 egg, 2 tablespoons firmly packed light brown sugar, 2 tablespoons dark corn syrup, 1 tablespoon melted butter and ½ teaspoon maple flavoring. Stir in 1 cup chopped pecans.

Prep Time: 30 minutes
Bake Time: 45 minutes

Sweet Potato Pecan Pie

Chess Pie

Actually, a custard pie, chess pie is believed to have originated in England. This vanilla-flavored version as well as lemon versions are popular in the South.

Crust

Classic CRISCO® Single Crust (recipe follows)

Filling

3 cups sugar

½ cup butter or margarine, softened

5 eggs, lightly beaten

3 tablespoons cornmeal

2 teaspoons vanilla

⅛ teaspoon salt

1 cup milk

1. For crust, prepare as directed. *Do not bake.* Heat oven to 325°F.

2. For filling, combine sugar and butter in large bowl. Beat at low speed of electric mixer until blended. Beat in eggs, cornmeal, vanilla and salt. Add milk. Beat at low speed until blended. Pour into unbaked pie crust.

3. Bake at 325°F for 1 hour to 1 hour 20 minutes or until filling is set. Cover edge of pie with foil, if necessary, to prevent overbrowning. *Do not overbake.* Cool to room temperature before serving. Refrigerate leftover pie.   *Makes 1 (10-inch) pie*

Classic Crisco® Single Crust

1⅓ cups all-purpose flour

½ teaspoon salt

½ CRISCO® Stick or ½ cup CRISCO® all-vegetable shortening

3 tablespoons cold water

1. Spoon flour into measuring cup and level. Combine flour and salt in medium bowl.

2. Cut in ½ cup shortening using pastry blender or 2 knives until all flour is blended to form pea-size chunks.

3. Sprinkle with water, 1 tablespoon at a time. Toss lightly with fork until dough forms a ball.

4. Press dough between hands to form 5- to 6-inch "pancake." Flour rolling surface and rolling pin lightly. Roll dough into circle. Trim circle 1 inch larger than upside-down pie plate. Carefully remove trimmed dough.

5. Fold dough into quarters. Unfold and press into pie plate. Fold edge under. Flute.

Makes 1 (9-inch) single crust

Acknowledgments

The publisher would like to thank the companies and organizations listed below for the use of their recipes and photographs in this publication.

ACH FOOD COMPANIES, INC.

Bob Evans®

ConAgra Foods®

Crisco is a registered trademark of The J.M. Smucker Company

Dole Food Company, Inc.

Eagle Brand® Sweetened Condensed Milk

Fleischmann's® Margarines and Spreads

Hershey Foods Corporation

The Hidden Valley® Food Products Company

Hormel Foods, Carapelli USA, LLC and Melting Pot Foods Inc.

McIlhenny Company (TABASCO® brand Pepper Sauce)

National Pork Board

Nestlé USA

Newman's Own, Inc.®

Reckitt Benckiser Inc.

The J.M. Smucker Company

Southeast United Dairy Industry Association, Inc.

Reprinted with permission of Sunkist Growers, Inc.

Texas Peanut Producers Board

Unilever Foods North America

METRIC CONVERSION CHART

VOLUME MEASUREMENTS (dry)

1/8 teaspoon = 0.5 mL
1/4 teaspoon = 1 mL
1/2 teaspoon = 2 mL
3/4 teaspoon = 4 mL
1 teaspoon = 5 mL
1 tablespoon = 15 mL
2 tablespoons = 30 mL
1/4 cup = 60 mL
1/3 cup = 75 mL
1/2 cup = 125 mL
2/3 cup = 150 mL
3/4 cup = 175 mL
1 cup = 250 mL
2 cups = 1 pint = 500 mL
3 cups = 750 mL
4 cups = 1 quart = 1 L

VOLUME MEASUREMENTS (fluid)

1 fluid ounce (2 tablespoons) = 30 mL
4 fluid ounces (1/2 cup) = 125 mL
8 fluid ounces (1 cup) = 250 mL
12 fluid ounces (1 1/2 cups) = 375 mL
16 fluid ounces (2 cups) = 500 mL

WEIGHTS (mass)

1/2 ounce = 15 g
1 ounce = 30 g
3 ounces = 90 g
4 ounces = 120 g
8 ounces = 225 g
10 ounces = 285 g
12 ounces = 360 g
16 ounces = 1 pound = 450 g

DIMENSIONS

1/16 inch = 2 mm
1/8 inch = 3 mm
1/4 inch = 6 mm
1/2 inch = 1.5 cm
3/4 inch = 2 cm
1 inch = 2.5 cm

OVEN TEMPERATURES

250°F = 120°C
275°F = 140°C
300°F = 150°C
325°F = 160°C
350°F = 180°C
375°F = 190°C
400°F = 200°C
425°F = 220°C
450°F = 230°C

BAKING PAN SIZES

Utensil	Size in Inches/Quarts	Metric Volume	Size in Centimeters
Baking or Cake Pan (square or rectangular)	8×8×2	2 L	20×20×5
	9×9×2	2.5 L	23×23×5
	12×8×2	3 L	30×20×5
	13×9×2	3.5 L	33×23×5
Loaf Pan	8×4×3	1.5 L	20×10×7
	9×5×3	2 L	23×13×7
Round Layer Cake Pan	8×1½	1.2 L	20×4
	9×1½	1.5 L	23×4
Pie Plate	8×1¼	750 mL	20×3
	9×1¼	1 L	23×3
Baking Dish or Casserole	1 quart	1 L	—
	1½ quart	1.5 L	—
	2 quart	2 L	—